JUST CAN'T CUT IT!

JUST CAN'T CUT IT!
QUILTS FROM FABULOUS FABRICS

❦ Pamela Mostek ❦

Martingale™
& COMPANY

Just Can't Cut It!: Quilts from Fabulous Fabrics
© 2003 by Pamela Mostek

Martingale & Company
20205 144th Avenue NE
Woodinville, WA 98072-8478
www.martingale-pub.com

Printed in China
08 07 06 05 04   8 7 6 5 4 3 2

Library of Congress Cataloging-in-Publication Data

Mostek, Pamela.
   Just can't cut it! : quilts from fabulous fabrics / Pamela Mostek.
      p. cm.
   ISBN 1-56477-449-X
   1. Patchwork—Patterns. 2. Quilting—Patterns. I. Title.

   TT835 .M693 2002
   746.46'041—dc21

                              2002151278

MISSION STATEMENT

Dedicated to providing quality products and service to inspire creativity.

CREDITS

President • Nancy J. Martin
CEO • Daniel J. Martin
Publisher • Jane Hamada
Editorial Director • Mary V. Green
Managing Editor • Tina Cook
Technical Editor • Ellen Pahl
Copy Editor • Karen Koll
Design Director • Stan Green
Illustrator • Robin Strobel
Cover and Text Designer • Trina Stahl
Photographer • Brent Kane

Dedication

To my father, Harold Sims. You're the best, always.

Acknowledgments

Thank you to everyone who helped and encouraged me as I developed the idea for and worked on this book. I would like to offer special thanks to:

Jean Van Bockel for rescuing me with her expert appliquéing and for sharing one of her great designs in this book.

Carol MacQuarrie for once again adding her expert machine quilting to my projects, and for her enthusiastic support of my colors and quilts.

Edi Dobbins for her help with piecing and for adding her good suggestions, even while flat on her back in a body cast!

Betty Labish and Genevieve Muench for adding their lovely appliqué to the book.

The staff at Martingale & Company for their support of my ideas and for bringing them to life in a book

Benartex, In The Beginning Fabrics, and Alexander Henry for supplying beautiful Just Can't Cut It fabric

And my family—my husband, Bob, and my daughters, Stacey and Rachel—for their ongoing enthusiasm and support of my ideas.

CONTENTS

❦

CONFESSIONS OF A FABRIC LOVER

OK, *I admit it*. When it comes to fabrics, I have no willpower! There are some fabrics I absolutely cannot resist. And I'm not particular. I adore all kinds of prints. Luscious cabbage rose patterns in garden shades of yellow and pink; giant paisleys in deep, rich tones of burgundy and purple; exotic Japanese prints with touches of shimmering gold; elegant, finely woven Liberty Tana Lawn fabric with that soft look of English dignity—I love them all! These beautiful, dramatic prints mysteriously call my name whenever I browse through the quilt shop. It's no use. I'm totally captivated by their charms.

I simply can't resist fabrics' dramatic artwork and rich shades of color. It's like a precious painting, I say to myself as I reverently carry a bolt of alluring fabric to the cutting table. Of course, I buy yards and yards—I am a fabric glutton. But what do I do with it? These, my favorite of all wonderful fabrics, are just too beautiful to cut into little pieces, so I save them. I add them to my gallery of fabrics, the ones I keep on display and admire, but never cut, of course.

Until now. This book is dedicated to those gorgeous fabrics that must be seen in large and dramatic pieces to be truly appreciated. No slicing these treasures into one-inch squares . . . only showing abundant pieces in all their beauty. Oh, there's a place for those tiny triangles and half-inch strips. They're a great accent for your special fabrics, but these masterpieces must be seen in their entirety to be appreciated.

If you, too, have been saving treasured fabrics for just the right quilt, try one of these designs that have been created just to show off your fabulous print. Or maybe you have more willpower than I do and you've passed up a truly unique fabric because you just didn't know how to use it. Now you can indulge yourself. Keep your eyes open for magnificent prints that will work perfectly in these designs.

No more will you have to look at gorgeous florals, paisleys, and plaids and say, "I just can't cut it!" Here you'll find a collection of projects designed with all of your favorite fabrics in mind. And I've included tips on how to select just the right companion fabrics to go with your Just Can't Cut It print so that it will truly shine in all its splendor.

So even though I must confess to still being very weak in the willpower department when it comes to bringing home these coveted fabrics, at least now I'm using them to create irresistible and dramatic quilts. And now that I've made the bold leap and taken a rotary cutter and ruler to my fabrics, I've discovered something very exciting— they are even lovelier made into just the right quilt than they are gracing the shelves of my sewing studio. Enjoy the book, and have fun cutting into those Just Can't Cut It fabrics!

Pam Mostek

THE OTHER FABRICS

You've found the perfect Just Can't Cut It fabric. Maybe it's a floral in soft shades of pink with a delicate hand-painted look. Or maybe it's a colorful, fun fruit print with a fanciful vintage look. Whatever it is, now that you've fallen in love with it, how do you make your quilt sparkle and show off that fabric jewel?

It's easy. It's all about the other fabrics that you select to go with your Just Can't Cut It print. By choosing the right ones, you can make sure your quilt is an absolute showstopper. You want to create your quilt so that the other fabrics complement your Just Can't Cut It fabric but don't compete with it. And just how do you do that? Simply keep in mind a few tips that I've discovered while "auditioning" other fabrics for the important role of accompanying my prized prints.

When you're fabric shopping, take your time making your selections. You'll be glad you did when you discover just the right plaid or geometric to accent your Just Can't Cut It print. Try leaning the bolt of your focal fabric against a shelf; then bring the companion fabrics you are considering and set them down next to the Just Can't Cut It fabric. Stand back and study it. Squint your eyes to see if it's just right. If your favorite fabric still shines through despite your squinted eyes, you have a winning combination.

To ensure a first-place lineup of fabrics, the following pages describe a few things to keep in mind as you make your selections. Take these tips along with you to the fabric store to help you decide whether or not you have a succesful companion fabric.

So Cut Already

Just remember the tips that follow when selecting your coordinating fabrics, and you'll be ready to put that fabric on your cutting mat. It's the moment you've been waiting for: cutting fabric! Then you can move on to the fun part of stitching it all together to create a truly unique Just Can't Cut It quilt. The fabrics will work together beautifully, and your project will be one that you can proudly display and enjoy in your home.

FABRIC LOVER'S TIP

In addition to the companion fabrics, the quilting, too, can add emphasis to your focal fabric. For the perfect finishing touch, refer to "Just Can't Cut It Quilting" on page 76 for more helpful information.

A LARGE-SCALE PRINT

꧁

If your Just Can't Cut It fabric is a large print, choose small-scale, subtle prints to complement it. Avoid middle-sized prints that will give less contrast in scale when compared to your focal fabric. A high contrast in print size adds emphasis to the fabric you aim to showcase. You want that gorgeous large-scale print to jump right out at you; a medium print will tend to minimize the impact of the larger one. Small-scale prints or geometrics will allow that Just Can't Cut It treasure to shine.

COLOR CHOICES

꧁

Companion colors work the same way as companion prints. You want to choose colors that won't compete with the colors in your Just Can't Cut It fabric. If you've fallen in love with an elegant floral in soft shades of pink, don't choose a bright or hot pink print to go with it, even if the scale of the print is right. The bright color will compete with the softer shades of the focal fabric. Sometimes, however, you need a color that is a little darker or lighter to add pizzazz. Try the stand-back-and-squint trick. If the color of your companion print shines brighter than your Just Can't Cut It print, keep searching!

KEEP IT SIMPLE

Keep your color palette simple. Rather than a wide array of companion colors, choose just a few hues from your Just Can't Cut It print. You can use the colored dots on the selvage edge to help you isolate potential companion colors. Usually I pick just two or three other colors and then use those colors to select coordinating fabrics. Although a lively group of different colored fabrics is the highlight of many great scrap quilts, too many colors will tend to compete with a Just Can't Cut It fabric. You don't need to limit yourself to just two or three fabrics, but they should all read as the same color. For example, if light green is one of my colors, I may choose several different light green fabrics, but they all still read as light green.

THE SURPRISE ELEMENT

Try the unexpected! Sometimes a surprising fabric choice gives a quilt that added sparkle. But once again, don't let the "surprise" element compete with your Just Can't Cut It fabric. You want the companion print to complement it nicely. One of my favorite combinations is a small plaid added to a luscious garden print. Or how about a touch of a woven homespun alongside an elegant Japanese print? You just can't tell until you try it!

DOUBLE DIAMONDS

Colorful diamonds make this quilt sparkle. On-point squares of a Just Can't Cut It print are surrounded
by an array of small diamonds in the sashing for an eye-catching diagonal movement across the quilt.
I used one of those charming retro kids' prints and surrounded it with bright, primary companion colors in the pieced sashing.
This quilt will work well in any color scheme, from subtle earth tones to glitzy holiday jewel tones.

Finished size: 69" x 85"

Materials

All yardages are based on 42"-wide fabric.

- 3⅞ yds. white fabric for sashing and sashing corner squares
- 3⅜ yds. Just Can't Cut It fabric for large diamonds
- 1¼ yds. *total* assorted brightly colored fabrics for small diamonds
- ⅝ yd. red fabric for sashing corner squares
- 5¼ yds. fabric for backing
- ¾ yd. fabric for binding
- 77" x 93" piece of batting

Cutting

From the assorted brightly colored fabrics, cut:

- 15 strips, 2½" x 42"

From the white fabric, cut:

- 30 strips, 2¾" x 42"
- 8 strips, 4" x 42"; crosscut into:
      160 rectangles, 2" x 4"
- 3 strips, 2½" x 42"; crosscut into:
      49 squares, 2½" x 2½"

From the red fabric, cut:

- 7 strips, 2½" x 42"; crosscut into:
      98 squares, 2½" x 2½"; cut each in half diagonally to make 196 triangles.

From the Just Can't Cut It fabric, cut:

- 8 strips, 9" x 42"; crosscut into:
      32 squares, 9" x 9"
- 4 squares, 18" x 18"; cut each twice diagonally to make 16 triangles.

From the binding fabric, cut:

- 8 strips, 2¾" x 42"

FABRIC LOVER'S TIP

If your Just Can't Cut It fabric is a light value print, choose a darker, contrasting color instead of white for the pieced sashing. Choose coordinating companion colors for the sashing squares.

Assembly

1. Sew the 15 strips of assorted bright colors between 30 white strips to make 15 strip sets. Press. Cut each strip set into 2½" segments to make a total of 240 segments.

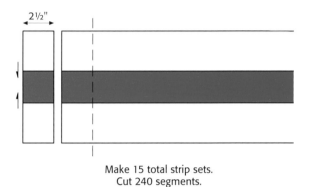

Make 15 total strip sets.
Cut 240 segments.

2. Select 3 segments from step 1, each with different colored center squares. Sew them together as shown in a stair-stepping technique.

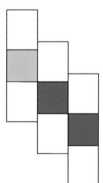

3. Add a 2" x 4" white rectangle to each end as shown. Press toward the white piece. Repeat to make a total of 80 multicolored sashing strips.

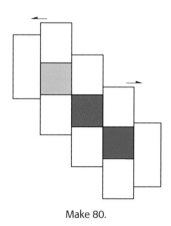

Make 80.

4. Using a see-through ruler and a rotary cutter, carefully trim the top, bottom, and sides of each unit, leaving a generous ¼" seam allowance on all edges. Set aside.

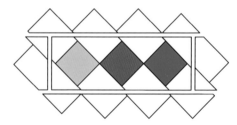

Trim, leaving a ¼" seam allowance.

5. To make the sashing corner squares, position 2 red triangles along opposite edges of a white square, right sides together. Stitch and press toward the triangles.

6. Add red triangles to the opposite sides in the same manner. Repeat to make a total of 49 sashing corner squares. Trim the "dog ear" seam allowances, and set aside.

Press and trim.
Make 49.

7. Arrange the 32 Just Can't Cut It squares and the sashing strips from step 4 in diagonal rows as shown at right. Sew the sashing strips and the red-and-white squares together in rows. Sew the short sashing strips and the Just Can't Cut It fabric squares together into rows, and then stitch the long sashing strips to the rows of blocks as shown.

8. Sew the side triangles of Just Can't Cut It fabric to the ends of each row, leaving the 4 corners without triangles. Sew the diagonal rows together. Press.

Finishing

1. Referring to "Finishing the Quilt Top" on pages 75–76, layer and baste the quilt. Quilt as desired. In the quilt in the photograph, the large squares were quilted with a spiral motif, starting in the center and winding out in larger circles. A smoke-colored monofilament thread was used so the stitching wouldn't detract from the fabric.

2. Add binding to the quilt, referring to "Binding" on pages 77–78.

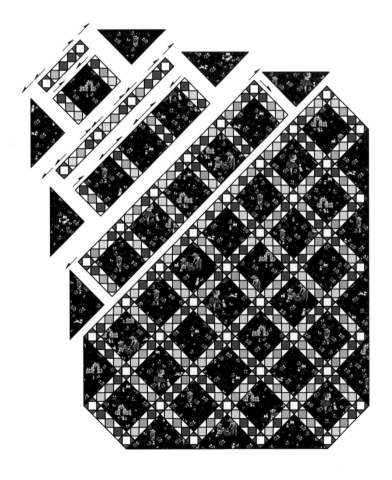

RIBBONS AND ROWS

Almost any Just Can't Cut It fabric will look dramatic when combined with rows of ribbon blocks arranged in a strippy setting. The ribbon blocks are strip-pieced and arranged in a zigzag pattern to perfectly complement a fantastic print. This is a perfect quilt to make when you want stunning results in a hurry.

Finished size: 46" x 60"

Materials

All yardages are based on 42"-wide fabric.

- 2 yds. Just Can't Cut It fabric for rows
- ¾ yd. each of 6 assorted coordinating fabrics for ribbon blocks
- 3 yds. fabric for backing
- ⅝ yd. fabric for facing
- 52" x 66" piece of batting
- 3½ yards of lightweight fusible interfacing (22"-wide)
- See-through ruler
- Water-soluble marker

Cutting

From the assorted coordinating fabrics, cut:
- 60 to 80 strips of varying widths, 1" to 2" x 42"

From the Just Can't Cut It fabric, cut:
- 5 lengthwise strips, 6½" x 60½"

From the facing fabric, cut:
- 6 strips, 3" x 42"

Ribbon Blocks

You will be using strip piecing and a stabilizer to make the ribbon blocks. You will need 60 blocks for the quilt.

1. Arrange the coordinating fabric strips of varying widths randomly and sew together to make 2 strip sets that are 28" x 40". The number of strips you will need depends on the varying widths. Just make sure the strip sets are at least 28" wide and 40" long. Press the seams in one direction.

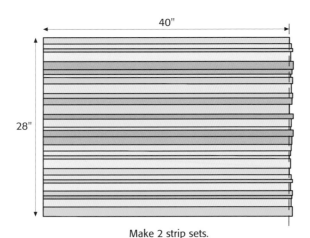

Make 2 strip sets.

2. Referring to the manufacturer's instructions, iron lightweight fusible interfacing to the wrong side of the strip sets. This will stabilize them so that you can easily cut your ribbon blocks on the bias without stretching.

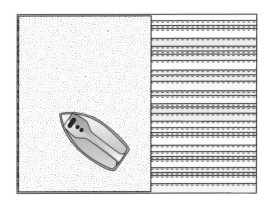

3. Using a see-through ruler and a water-soluble marker, draw a line on the bias grain of one of the strip sets.

4. Use the line drawn in step 3 to measure and draw repeated diagonal lines every 4½" through the length of the strip set. Repeat to draw diagonal lines in the opposite direction, making a diagonal grid on the strip set. Cut along the drawn lines.

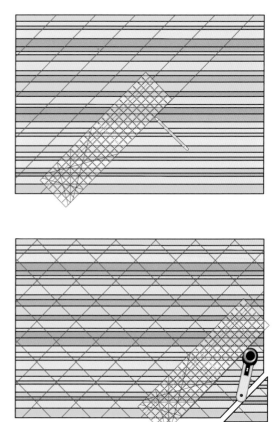

5. Repeat to mark and cut the second strip set. Because you will have extra blocks, you can choose your favorites and save the others for another project.

Cut at least 60 blocks.

Assembly

1. Sew the ribbon blocks together to make 4 vertical rows of 15 blocks each. Alternate the direction of the blocks to create a vertical zigzag pattern as shown. Press.

Make 4.

2. Beginning with a Just Can't Cut It print strip, sew together the 4 rows of ribbon blocks and 5 strips of the print fabric in an alternating pattern. Press the seam allowances toward the print strips.

Finishing

1. Referring to "Finishing the Quilt Top" on pages 75–76, layer and baste the quilt. Quilt in the seam lines between the rows. To accentuate the vertical lines of the quilt, quilt a vertical pattern in the ribbon rows, rather than an overall pattern. In the Just Can't Cut It print rows, try using the print as your quilting guide, referring to "Just Can't Cut It Quilting" on page 76.

2. In order to maintain the emphasis on the vertical look of the quilt, add facings to the edges rather than a binding. A traditional binding would add a horizontal design element at the top and bottom of the quilt. Measure the length of the quilt through the center. Piece the facing strips and cut two to the length of the quilt. With right sides together and raw edges matching, pin facing strips to the sides and sew with a ¼" seam.

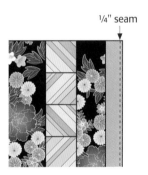

¼" seam

3. From the front of the quilt, press the strips outward and topstitch ⅛" from the seam through all the layers.

⅛" from seam

Topstitch through all layers.

4. Fold the facing to the back of the quilt so that a slight edge of the quilt top rolls to the back. Press with steam. Turn the raw edges under ¼" and hand stitch them to the back.

Quilt back

5. Measure the width of the quilt through the center. Cut the top and bottom facings 2" longer than the width of the quilt. Repeat steps 2 through 4 to add facings but with 1" extending beyond each edge. Fold in the excess at each end and hem in place.

I LOVE LIBERTY

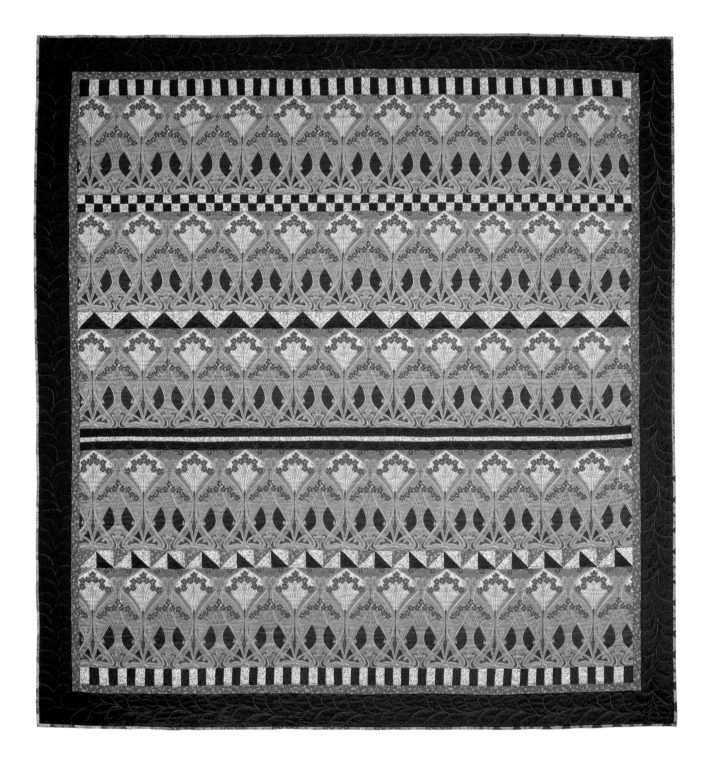

I'm a great fan of Liberty of London fabrics with their fabulous colors and designs and their almost silk-like feel. I fell in love with the spectacular Just Can't Cut It fabric in this quilt. With its sophisticated colors and art deco look, it definitely ranks high on my most-loved list! This quilt design is very easily adapted to any wonderful fabric, as you can see in the variation on page 27. Fabrics with floral designs or other swirly, curving lines will contrast best with the bold, graphic pieced rows.

Finished size: 74" x 77½"

Materials

All yardages are based on 42"-wide fabric.

- 3½ yds.* Just Can't Cut It fabric for the rows
- 2 yds. purple fabric for the pieced rows and border
- 1 yd. light print fabric for the pieced rows
- ⅝ yd. rose print fabric for the pieced rows and border
- 5½ yds. fabric for backing
- ¾ yd. fabric for binding
- 82" x 85" piece of batting

This includes extra fabric for matching the print.

FABRIC LOVER'S TIP

When selecting the fabric for the outer borders, I recommend using one of the fabrics from the pieced rows. You don't want the border fabric to compete with the Just Can't Cut It fabric. You could also look for a print in a complementary color, but make sure that it is not a busy, large-scale, or competing print.

Cutting

From the purple fabric, cut:

- 4 strips, 1½" x 42"
- 16 strips, 1½" x 11"
- 12 strips, 1½" x 10"
- 2 strips, 2½" x 42"; crosscut into:
    16 rectangles, 2½" x 4½"
- 2 strips, 2⅞" x 42"; crosscut into:
    16 squares, 2⅞" x 2⅞"
- 8 strips, each 4½" x 42"

From the light print fabric, cut:

- 16 strips, 1½" x 11"
- 12 strips, 1½" x 10"
- 2 strips, 2½" x 42"; crosscut into:
    32 squares, 2½" x 2½"
- 2 strips, 1" x 42"
- 3 strips, 2⅞" x 42"; crosscut into:
    32 squares, 2⅞" x 2⅞"

From the rose fabric, cut:

- 2 strips, 2⅞" x 42"; crosscut into:
    16 squares, 2⅞" x 2⅞"
- 8 strips, 1½" x 42"

From the Just Can't Cut It fabric, cut:

- 10 strips, 11½" x 42"

From the binding fabric, cut:

- 8 strips, 2¾" x 42"

Pieced Rows

The pieced rows are numbered 1 through 6, beginning at the top of the quilt. Refer to the diagram on page 25 as you assemble the quilt.

1. **Rows 1 and 6:** Use the 16 purple and 16 light print strips, 1½" x 11". Alternating colors, sew the 32 strips into a strip set. Press toward the purple strips. Cut the strip set into 4 segments, each 2½" wide.

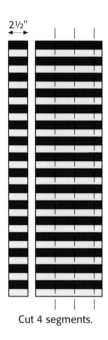

Cut 4 segments.

2. Join the 4 segments in pairs end to end to make row 1 and row 6. Measure each row. It may be necessary to take in or let out seams slightly so that each row measures 64½". Set the rows aside.

3. **Row 2:** Use the 12 purple and 12 light print strips, each 1½" x 10". Alternating purple and light print strips, sew the 24 strips into a strip set. Press toward the purple strips. Cut the strips into 6 segments, each 1½" wide.

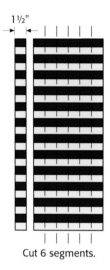

Cut 6 segments.

4. Sew the segments together end to end to make 2 rows with 3 segments in each row. Remove 8 squares from the end of each row to leave 64 squares in each. Press. Adjust seams if necessary, so that the rows measure 64½". Alternating colors, sew the 2 rows together to make a checkerboard row. Press and set aside.

5. **Row 3:** With a pencil and see-through ruler, draw a diagonal line on the wrong side of 32 light print squares, each 2½" x 2½". With right sides together, position 16 squares on the ends of 16 purple rectangles. Stitch on the drawn line. Trim the seam and press.

6. Repeat to add remaining 16 squares to the opposite ends of the purple units.

Make 16.

7. Matching the short ends, sew the 16 units from step 6 together in a row. Adjust seams, if necessary, so that the row measures 64½". Set aside.

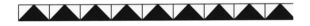

8. **Row 4:** Join 4 purple strips, each 1½" x 42", end to end in pairs; trim each to measure 64½". Join 2 light print strips, each 1" x 42", end to end; trim to 64½".

9. Sew a purple strip to either side of the light print strip and press seams toward the purple. Set aside.

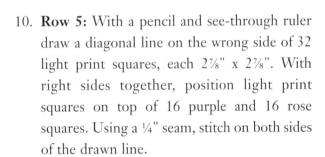

10. **Row 5:** With a pencil and see-through ruler draw a diagonal line on the wrong side of 32 light print squares, each 2⅞" x 2⅞". With right sides together, position light print squares on top of 16 purple and 16 rose squares. Using a ¼" seam, stitch on both sides of the drawn line.

11. Cut on the drawn line and press toward the darker fabric.

Make 32 total.

12. Position the purple and rose triangles as shown and sew together the 32 triangle squares. Adjust the seams, if necessary, so that the row measures 64½". Press and set aside.

Assembly

1. Sew the 10 Just Can't Cut It strips together end to end in pairs to make 5 strips. Carefully match the print as you join the strips. Trim each of the 5 strips to 64½", taking care that the designs align vertically if desired.

2. Assemble the Just Can't Cut It strips and pieced rows 1–6 as shown. Press seams toward the strips.

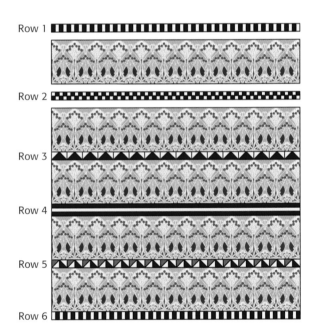

3. Referring to "Adding Borders" on pages 74–75, add the narrow (1½") rose border and the wide (4½") purple border to the quilt.

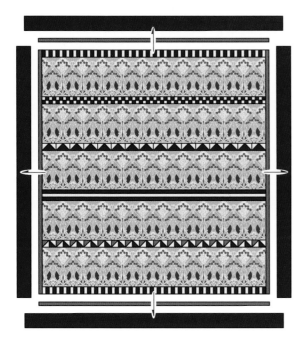

Finishing

1. Referring to "Finishing the Quilt Top" on pages 75–76, layer and baste the quilt.

2. Machine quilt in the seam lines between rows and as desired around the fabric pattern. Refer to "Just Can't Cut It Quilting" on page 76 for quilting suggestions.

3. Add the binding to the quilt, referring to "Binding" on pages 77–78.

ANOTHER LOOK for "I LOVE LIBERTY"

I Love Pink, 48" x 65½"

It's very easy to adapt "I Love Liberty" to fit your favorite Just Can't Cut It fabric. For a delicate, springlike look, I've sewn it in shades of pink and peach with a Just Can't Cut It fabric of blooming tulips.

You can also modify the size of the quilt. To adjust the width, remember to make the width of the center without the borders divisible by four so that the pieced rows will fit evenly. In this quilt, the strips were cut from a single width of fabric, but since the width needed to be divisible by four, they were trimmed to 40½".

You can make the horizontal strips any height or width that will complement your print. Just follow the instructions for "Adding the Borders" on pages 74–75 to determine the border length.

JOSIE'S QUILT

Before my first granddaughter, Josie, was born, I dipped into my beloved collection of fun Just Can't Cut It kids' prints and designed this baby quilt to show off the Red Riding Hood fabric. I also whipped up a second quilt from the same design but without the appliquéd hearts. And it was all pink . . . of course! For a baby quilt, this would be soft and lovely made up in flannels or brushed homespuns, too.

Finished size: 37½" x 37½"

Materials

All yardages are based on 42"-wide fabric.

- 1 yd. Just Can't Cut It fabric for center square and outer border
- ½ yd. red print fabric for border
- ⅜ yd. off-white fabric for checkerboard and narrow border
- ⅜ yd. light green fabric for corner triangles
- ¼ yd. red fabric for checkerboard
- Scraps of red and dark pink fabric for appliqué
- 1⅜ yds. fabric for backing
- ½ yd. fabric for binding
- 42" x 42" piece of batting
- ¼ yd. fusible web
- See-through ruler
- Water-soluble marker
- Template plastic

Cutting

From the red fabric, cut:
- 3 strips, 1½" x 42"; crosscut into:
    12 strips, 1½" x 10"

From the off-white fabric, cut:
- 6 strips, 1½" x 42"; crosscut into:
    12 strips, 1½" x 10"
    4 strips, 1½" x 9¾"
    4 strips, 1½" x 11¾"

From the Just Can't Cut It fabric, cut:
- 1 square, 23½" x 23½"
- 2 strips, 2" x 35"
- 2 strips, 2" x 37½"

From the light green fabric, cut:
- 2 squares, 9¾" x 9¾"

From the red print fabric, cut:
- 4 strips, 3½" x 42"; crosscut into:
    4 strips, 3½" x 11¾"
    4 strips, 3½" x 17¾"

From the binding fabric, cut:
- 5 strips, 2¾" x 42"

Assembly

1. Alternating the 1½" x 10" strips of red and off-white fabrics, sew the 24 pieces together into a strip set. Press seams toward the red strips. Crosscut the strip set into 4 checkerboard strips, 1½" wide.

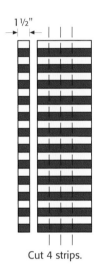

Cut 4 strips.

2. With a seam ripper, remove 1 off-white square from the ends of 2 checkerboard strips, and set them aside. Sew the strips to the sides of the center square of Just Can't Cut It fabric. Press toward the center square.

3. Sew the 2 off-white squares that you removed in step 1 to the red squares at the ends of the 2 remaining checkerboard strips. Sew these checkerboard strips to the top and bottom of the center square. Press.

4. Sew two 1½" x 9¾" off-white strips to the sides of each of the two 9¾" light green squares; press toward the light green square. Sew a 1½" x 11¾" off-white strip to the top and bottom of each square. Press. Add the 3½" x 11¾" red print strips to the sides and the 3½" x 17¾" red print strips to the top and bottom of each of the units. Press toward the red print strips.

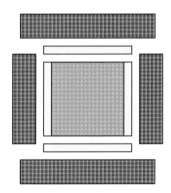

5. Using a see-through ruler and water-soluble marker, draw a diagonal line from corner to corner on each of the blocks from step 4. Use a rotary cutter and ruler to cut along the drawn line, dividing each block into 2 triangles.

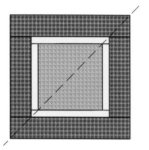 

6. Sew 2 of the triangle units to opposite sides of the center square from step 3. Press. Sew the remaining triangle units to the remaining sides. Press.

7. Sew the 2" x 35" Just Can't Cut It border strips to the sides. Press. Sew the 2" x 37½" strips to the top and bottom. Press.

Appliqué Hearts

1. To make heart templates, trace the large and small heart patterns from page 33 onto template plastic and cut out.

2. Trace around the templates onto the paper side of the fusible web. Trace 8 small hearts and 4 large hearts. Following the manufacturer's instructions, iron the fusible web onto the wrong sides of the scraps of pink and red fabric. Cut out and remove the paper backing. Fuse the hearts to the corners of the quilt, referring to the photo for placement.

3. Use machine appliqué or a hand blanket stitch around the edges of the hearts. For machine appliqué, use a narrow satin stitch or a decorative stitch, and sew with a stabilizer underneath to avoid puckers. Remove the stabilizer after stitching.

Finishing

1. Referring to "Finishing the Quilt Top" on pages 75–76, layer and baste the quilt. Machine quilt as desired.

2. Add binding to the quilt, referring to "Binding" on pages 77–78.

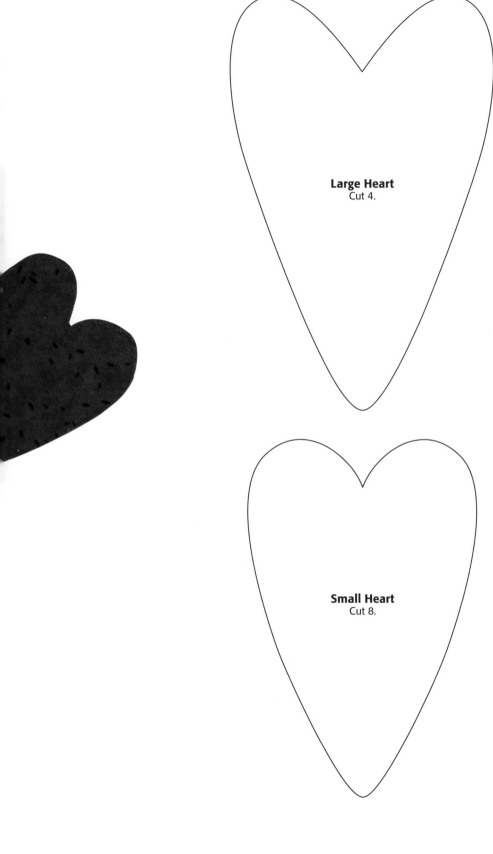

Large Heart
Cut 4.

Small Heart
Cut 8.

GARDEN LATTICE

Gorgeous fantasy flowers are blooming everywhere on this delightful quilt. In order to make the most of your Just Can't Cut It print, try using it everywhere you can in the project: center squares, borders, even backing and binding. When you wrap up in this irresistible quilt, you'll be surrounded by delightful blooms!

Finished size: 61" x 76"

Materials

All yardages are based on 42"-wide fabric.

- 4 yds. Just Can't Cut It fabric for quilt background
- 1⅛ yds. blue fabric for lattice sashing and sashing squares
- ⅝ yd. yellow fabric for lattice sashing
- ¼ yd. dark green fabric for lattice sashing squares
- 4 yds. fabric for backing
- ¾ yd. fabric for binding
- 67" x 82" piece of batting

Cutting

From the Just Can't Cut It fabric, cut:
- 12 squares, 12½" x 12½"
- 23 strips, 1" x 42"; crosscut 21 into:
    - 62 strips, 1" x 12½"
    - 7 strips, 2½" x 42"
    - 7 strips, 4½" x 42"

From the blue fabric, cut:
- 34 strips, 1" x 42"; crosscut 27 into:
    - 40 rectangles, 1" x 2½"
    - 40 rectangles, 1" x 3½"
    - 62 strips, 1" x 12½"

From the yellow fabric, cut:
- 11 strips, 1½" x 42"; crosscut into:
    - 31 strips, 1½" x 12½"

From the dark green fabric, cut:
- 3 strips, 1½" x 42"; crosscut 2 strips into:
    - 20 rectangles, 1½" x 2½"

From the binding fabric, cut:
- 7 strips, 2¾" x 42"

Assembly

1. To make the 31 sashing units, sew together as shown 62 Just Can't Cut It strips, each 1" x 12½"; 62 blue strips, each 1" x 12½"; and the 31 yellow strips, each 1½" x 12½". Press all the seams in one direction.

Make 31.

2. Sew 3 Just Can't Cut It squares between 4 sashing units from step 1. Press toward the squares. Repeat to make a total of 4 rows.

Make 4.

3. To make the sashing squares, sew the 1½" x 42" dark green strip between two 1" x 42" Just Can't Cut It strips. Cut each strip set into 1" segments for a total of 40 segments.

NOTE: *If you don't get 40 segments from your strip set, cut two 1" x 6" strips of Just Can't Cut It fabric, and one 1½" x 6" dark green strip to make an additional short strip set.*

Cut 40 segments.

4. Sew 2 segments from step 3 together with a dark green rectangle, two 1" x 2½" blue rectangles, and two 1" x 3½" blue rectangles as shown. The square should measure 3½" x 3½". Repeat to make 20 sashing squares.

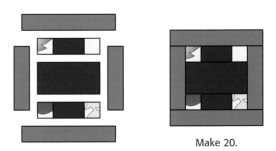

Make 20.

5. Sew the remaining 15 sashing units from step 1 between the 20 sashing squares as shown to make 5 rows. Press toward the corner squares.

Make 5.

6. Sew together the rows from step 2 and step 5 as shown.

7. Refer to "Adding Borders" on pages 74–75. Measure the quilt top through the center to determine the length. Piece the 2½"-wide Just Can't Cut It border strips and cut them to the length needed for the quilt sides. Add borders to the sides. Press toward the borders. Repeat for the top and bottom borders.

8. Repeat step 7 for the 1" blue borders. Press.

9. Repeat step 7 to add the 4½" Just Can't Cut It borders. Press.

Finishing

1. Referring to "Finishing the Quilt Top" on pages 75–76, layer and baste the quilt. Quilt as desired.

2. Add binding to the quilt, referring to "Binding" on pages 77–78.

GRANDPA'S COZY QUILT

Curling up in this cuddly flannel quilt is almost as good as a big hug from Grandpa. Using this striking paisley flannel, I designed this cozy quilt just for him. It's a variation of Garden Lattice, page 34, but with a little less piecing, which is perfect for using a Just Can't Cut It flannel. Not quite as warm and wonderful as Grandpa's hugs, but close!

Finished size: 64" x 82"

Materials

All yardages are based on 42"-wide flannel fabric.

- 3 yds. Just Can't Cut It flannel for background and border
- 1⅛ yds. cream flannel for sashing
- 1 yd. green flannel for sashing
- ⅞ yd. rose print flannel for sashing squares
- 5 yds. flannel for backing
- ¾ yd. flannel for binding
- 72" x 90" piece of batting

FABRIC LOVER'S TIP

With all the beautifully colored flannels on the market, you won't have any trouble finding a Just Can't Cut It flannel for your cozy quilt. Select your favorite and use it just as you would quality quilting cotton.

Cutting

From the Just Can't Cut It flannel, cut:
- 12 squares, 12½" x 12½"
- 21 strips, 1½" x 42"; crosscut into:
  62 strips, 1½" x 12½"
- 7 strips, 2½" x 42"

From the green flannel, cut:
- 11 strips, 2½" x 42"; crosscut into:
  31 strips, 2½" x 12½"

From the cream flannel, cut:
- 21 strips, 1½" x 42"; crosscut into:
  62 strips, 1½" x 12½"

From the rose print flannel, cut:
- 4 strips, 6½" x 42"; crosscut into:
  20 squares, 6½" x 6½"

From the binding fabric, cut:
- 8 strips, 2¾" x 42"

Assembly

1. To make the 31 sashing units, sew together as shown the 1½" x 12½" Just Can't Cut It strips, the green strips, and the cream strips. Press all the seams in one direction.

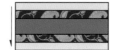

Make 31.

2. Sew 3 Just Can't Cut It squares between 4 sashing units from step 1. Press toward the squares. Repeat to make a total of 4 rows.

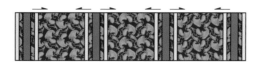

Make 4.

3. Sew the remaining 15 sashing units from step 1 between the 20 rose print sashing squares as shown to make 5 rows. Press toward the sashing squares.

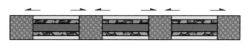

Make 5.

4. Sew together the rows from steps 2 and 3 and press.

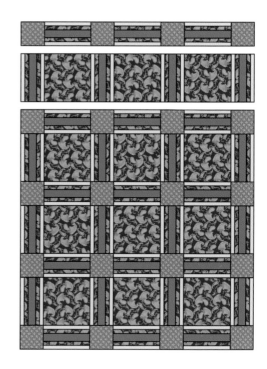

5. Measure the quilt through the center to determine the length. Piece the 2½" side border strips and trim to the correct measurement. Sew to the sides of the quilt and press toward the borders. Measure the quilt through the center to determine the width. Piece the remaining border strips and trim to the correct width. Sew to the top and bottom. Press.

Finishing

1. Referring to "Finishing the Quilt Top" on pages 75–76, layer and baste the quilt. Quilt as desired.

2. Add binding to the quilt, referring to "Binding" on pages 77–78.

FABRIC LOVER'S TIPS

Don't quilt a flannel quilt too heavily. This will keep it softer and cozier. Heavy quilting will make it stiffer and flatter.

Machine quilting along seam lines, known as "stitching in the ditch," works very well with flannel quilts. To keep your in-the-ditch quilting invisible, try using monofilament on the top and regular machine thread in the bobbin. Use clear monofilament for light fabrics and smoke-colored for dark fabrics.

KENSINGTON SQUARE

I couldn't resist this large, richly colored Just Can't Cut It print in lovely shades of brown, cream, and burgundy; but Kensington Square will be fabulous in your favorite print and colors, too. What a dramatic touch this luscious quilt will add to a bed. The Celtic-inspired appliqué accentuates the elegance!

Finished size: 86" x 86"

Materials

All yardages are based on 42"-wide fabric.

- 4¾ yds. Just Can't Cut It fabric for the center and borders
- 1⅛ yds. green dotted fabric for third, fourth, and fifth narrow borders
- ⅞ yd. variegated burgundy-and-rose fabric for triangle border and unpieced accent border
- ¾ yd. burgundy fabric for appliqué
- ⅝ yd. light green fabric for triangle border and appliqué leaves
- ⅝ yd. green plaid for center triangles
- ⅜ yd. rose fabric for appliqué
- ⅜ yd. burgundy plaid for second narrow border
- ¼ yd. burgundy print for first narrow border
- 8 yds. for backing
- ⅞ yd. for binding
- 94" x 94" piece of batting
- Freezer paper
- ½" bias press bars

Cutting

From the green plaid fabric, cut:
- 2 squares, 18½" x 18½"; cut in half diagonally once to yield 4 triangles

From the Just Can't Cut It fabric, cut:
- 1 square, 24½" x 24½"
- 12 strips, 4½" x 42"
- 9 strips, 8½" x 42"

From the burgundy print fabric, cut:
- 2 strips, 1½" x 34½"
- 2 strips, 1½" x 36½"

From the light green fabric, cut:
- 3 strips, 2⅞" x 42"; crosscut into:
  36 squares, 2⅞" x 2⅞"
- 5 strips, 1½" x 42"
- 4 squares, 2½" x 2½"

From the burgundy-and-rose variegated fabric, cut:
- 3 strips, 2⅞" x 42"; crosscut into:
  36 squares, 2⅞" x 2⅞"
- 6 strips, 2½" x 42"

From the burgundy plaid fabric, cut:
- 5 strips, 1½" x 42"

From the green dotted fabric, cut:
- 23 strips, 1½" x 42"

From the binding fabric, cut:
- 9 strips, 2¾" x 2¾"

Assembly

1. With right sides together, sew 2 green plaid triangles to opposite sides of the Just Can't Cut It square. Press toward the square. Add the remaining 2 green plaid triangles; press. Note that the triangles are cut slightly oversize to allow for squaring up after the appliqué is added.

TRIANGLE TIP

Before sewing the green triangles onto the center square, fold each in half and crease lightly to mark the center points of the long edges. Fold the square in half and make creases at the center point on each side. Match the creases and pin before sewing.

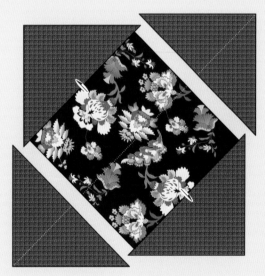

Sew triangles on each side of large square, matching centers.

2. Referring to "Cutting Bias Strips" on page 74, cut about 220" of 2"-wide bias strips from the burgundy fabric for appliqué. Using ½" bias press bars and referring to "Appliqué Vines" on page 74, make bias tubes to outline the leaf shapes. You will need 4 tubes, each approximately 51" long.

3. Cut approximately 60" of bias strips from the rose fabric for the appliquéd small circles. Join the strips end to end and make a bias tube as in step 2. You will need a tube approximately 12" to 15" long for each circle.

4. Using the pattern on page 48, trace 12 of the center leaf shapes onto the dull side of freezer paper. Iron the shiny side to the wrong side of the light green fabric and cut out, adding a ¼" seam allowance. Using the placement guide below and the quilt layout on page 45, position the leaf centers onto the quilt top and pin in place. Baste the leaves to the background using a running stitch in the seam allowance around the outer edges. This will hold the leaves in place, and the bias tubes will cover the raw edges.

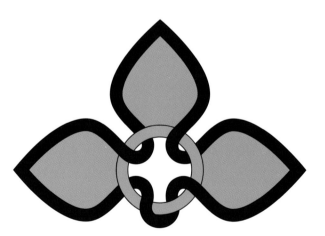

Placement Guide

5. Position the bias tubes for the circle and leaves around the leaf centers. Begin and end each strip underneath the other strip so that the raw edges are hidden underneath the appliqué. Pin generously and appliqué in place, referring to "Appliqué" on pages 72–74. Remove the freezer paper from behind the leaves. Trim and square up the top to measure 34½" square.

6. To add the first narrow border, sew a 1½" x 34½" burgundy print strip to each side of the center unit. Press toward the narrow border. Sew a 1½" x 36½" strip to each of the remaining sides. Press.

7. With a pencil and see-through ruler, draw a diagonal line on the wrong side of the 36 light green 2⅞" squares. With right sides together, position the green squares on top of the 36 variegated burgundy-and-rose squares. Using a ¼" seam, sew on either side of the drawn lines.

8. Cut along the drawn lines and press the seam toward the darker fabric.

Make 72.

9. Sew the triangle square units as shown into 4 border strips with 18 squares in each. If you are using variegated fabric, position the squares so that they go from a darker to lighter shade in a pleasing manner. Each border strip should measure 34½". If it does not, let out or take in the seams very slightly until it does.

Make 4.

10. Sew 2 of the strips from step 9 to the sides of the center unit from step 6. Press toward the center. Sew the 4 light green 2½" squares to the ends of the 2 remaining strips and press. Sew the strips to the top and bottom of the center unit. Press.

11. Piece the light green strips as needed; trim 2 strips to 40½" and 2 strips to 42½". Sew the 40½" strips to the sides of the center unit and press. Sew the 42½" strips to the top and bottom. Press.

FABRIC LOVER'S TIP

When you need to piece strips of fabric together, a diagonal seam is less noticeable than a straight seam. See "Adding Borders" on pages 72–73 for instructions on how to stitch a diagonal seam.

---

12. For the second narrow border, piece the burgundy plaid strips; trim 2 strips to 42½" and 2 strips to 44½". Sew the shorter strips to the sides of the center unit. Press toward the burgundy plaid strips. Sew the remaining 2 strips to the top and bottom. Press.

13. Piece and trim 2 Just Can't Cut It strips to 4½" x 44½" and sew them to the sides of the center unit; piece and trim 2 strips to 4½" x 52½" and sew them to the top and bottom.

14. For the third narrow border, piece and trim 2 green dotted strips to 1½" x 52½" and sew them to the sides; piece and trim 2 strips to 1½" x 54½" and sew them to the top and bottom.

15. Piece and trim 2 variegated burgundy-and-rose strips to 2½" x 54½" and sew them to the sides; piece and trim 2 strips to 2½" x 58½" and sew them to the top and bottom.

16. For the fourth narrow border, piece and trim 2 green dotted strips to 1½" x 58½" and sew them to the sides of the quilt; piece and trim 2 strips to 1½" x 60½" and sew them to the top and bottom.

17. Piece and trim 2 Just Can't Cut It strips to 4½" x 60½" and sew them to the sides; piece and trim 2 strips to 4½" x 68½" and sew them to the top and bottom.

18. For the fifth narrow border, piece and trim 2 green dotted strips to 1½" x 68½" and sew them to the sides; piece and trim 2 strips to 1½" x 70½" and sew them to the top and bottom.

19. Piece and trim 2 Just Can't Cut It strips to 8½" x 70½" and sew them to the sides; piece and trim 2 strips to 8½" x 86½" and sew them to the top and bottom.

Finishing

1. Referring to "Finishing the Quilt Top" on pages 75–76, layer and baste the quilt. Machine quilt as desired, referring to "Just Can't Cut It Quilting" on page 76 to highlight the fabric with quilting.

2. Referring to "Binding" on pages 77–78, bind the quilt.

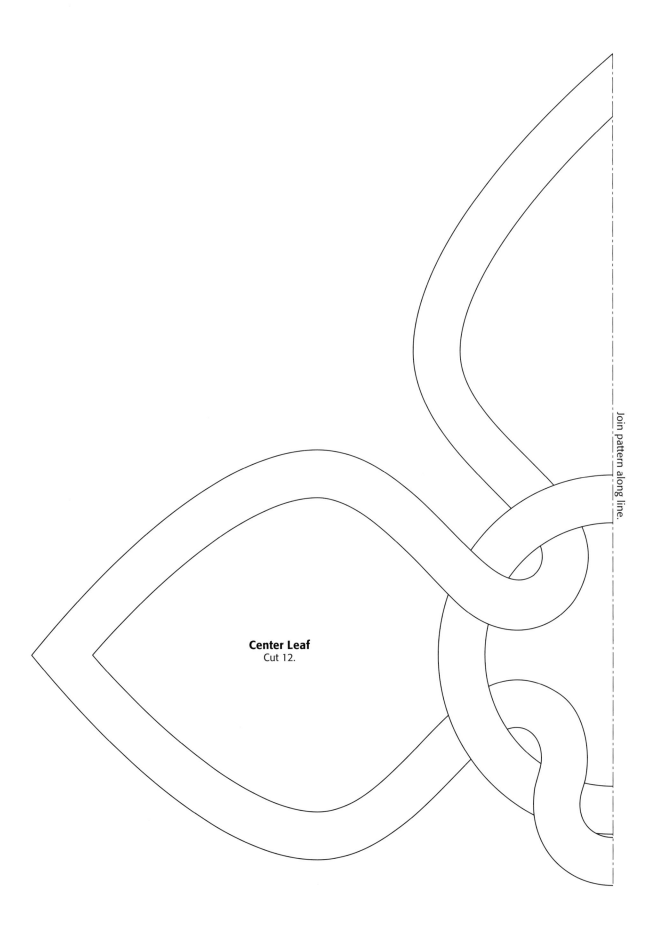

Center Leaf
Cut 12.

Join pattern along line.

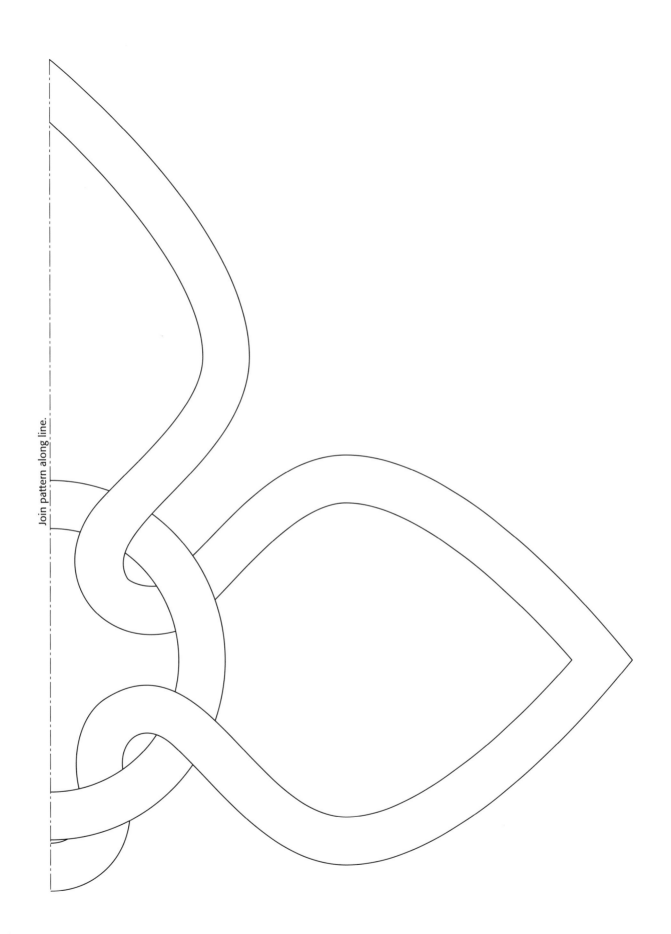

Join pattern along line.

JAPANESE JEWELS

Here's your chance to use more than one Just Can't Cut It fabric in your quilt.
In fact, you might just try using a whole collection! This quilt is perfect for showcasing those gorgeous Japanese fabrics
I can't resist, but it would work well with any treasured fabrics you've been collecting.

Finished size: 47" x 47"

Materials

All yardages are based on 42"-wide fabric.

- 4 to 5½ yds. *total* of 12 to 15 assorted Just Can't Cut It fabrics for blocks
- 1⅜ yds. black fabric for sashing and binding
- ⅝ yd. gray print fabric for border
- ⅜ yd. gold print fabric for border
- 3¼ yds. fabric for backing
- 53" x 53" piece of batting
- ½" bias press bar
- Monofilament quilting thread

FABRIC LOVER'S TIP

The blocks in this quilt are a good option when you don't have a lot of any one special fabric; they're perfect for bundles of unique fat quarters—the ones you just had to have but didn't know what you'd make with them!

Cutting

From the Just Can't Cut It Fabrics, cut:
- 9 pieces, 13" x 7" (piece #1)
- 9 pieces, 13" x 13" (piece #2)
- 9 pieces, 13" x 6" (piece #3)
- 9 pieces, 9" x 4" (piece #4)
- 9 pieces, 11" x 11" (piece #5)

From the gold print fabric, cut:
- 2 strips, 4½" x 42"

From the gray print fabric, cut:
- 4 strips, 4½" x 42"

From the black fabric, cut:
- 12 strips, 2" x 42"
- 5 strips, 2¾" x 42"

Blocks

You will be making nine paper-pieced blocks using your assorted Just Can't Cut It fabrics. Select five different fabrics for each block. Set your machine stitch length shorter than usual.

1. Enlarge and make 9 copies of the paper-piecing pattern on page 55. For each block, begin by pinning piece 1 in position on the blank side of the paper pattern. To make sure you have positioned the piece so that it completely covers section 1 on your paper pattern, hold it up to the light and adjust if necessary.

2. With right sides together, align the edge of piece 2 with the edge of piece 1 and pin in place. With the paper side up, stitch on the line. Begin and end your stitching a few stitches before and after the line.

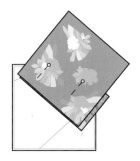
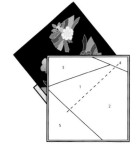

3. Trim the seam allowance to ¼", flip so that the right side is up, and press with a dry iron.

4. Repeat steps 1 through 3, stitching each piece in order until you have added all 5 pieces to the block. Trim around the finished block to the ¼" seam allowance. To stabilize the edges and prevent stretching, leave the paper attached until after the blocks have been sewn together.

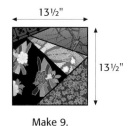

13½"

13½"

Make 9.

5. Repeat steps 1 through 4 to complete all 9 blocks.

Assembly

1. Rotate the blocks until you are pleased with the arrangement of the fabrics and place them in 3 rows of 3 blocks each.

2. Sew the blocks together in rows; press seams in opposite directions from row to row. Sew the rows together. From the back of the quilt, carefully tear away the paper on the blocks. Press.

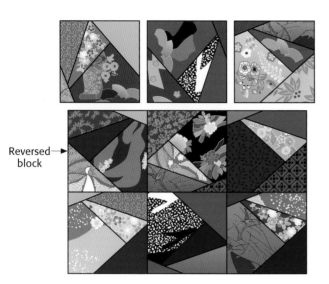

Reversed → block

3. For the borders, sew a gold strip to a gray strip, stitching a diagonal seam. (See "Adding Borders" on pages 74–75 for information on sewing a diagonal seam.) Repeat for the remaining gold strip and a second gray strip.

FABRIC LOVER'S TIP

A design wall is the best way to view your blocks before you sew them together. Cover a large frame or piece of foam-core board with flannel or batting and hang it on the wall. Move your blocks around until you're happy with the arrangement.

4. Trim 1 gray print strip so that it measures 4½" x 39½" and sew to the right side of the center unit. Press toward the border.

5. Position a gray-and-gold pieced border strip along the left side of the unit, placing the diagonal seam approximately 12" from the lower left corner. Trim the border strip to 39½". Sew it to the quilt top and press toward the border.

6. Position the diagonal seam of the remaining pieced border strip approximately 15" from the upper left corner of the unit. Trim the border strip to measure 4½" x 47½" and sew to the top. Press.

7. Piece and trim the remaining gray border strip so that it measures 4½" x 47½". Sew to the bottom and press.

8. Using diagonal seams, sew together the 12 black strips, 2" x 42", joining the short ends to make 1 long strip. With wrong sides together, press this strip in half lengthwise.

9. Refer to "Appliqué Vines" on page 74 for instructions on using the bias press bar to make 1 long tube from the strip. Cut this tube into 10 sashing strips, each 47½" in length.

10. Referring to the quilt layout below, carefully center and pin a black sashing strip over each of the seams between the blocks and at the borders. Using a machine appliqué stitch, sew along both edges of the strips. Position and sew 1 extra horizontal and vertical sashing strip to the quilt as shown.

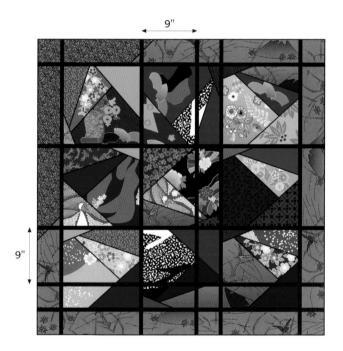

Finishing

1. Referring to "Finishing the Quilt Top" on pages 75–76, layer and baste the quilt. Use transparent monofilament thread on light fabrics and smoke-colored monofilament on dark fabrics. Quilt lightly with a meandering stitch. Quilt over the appliquéd sashing strips as you quilt the rest of the top.

2. Add binding to the quilt, referring to "Binding" on pages 77–78.

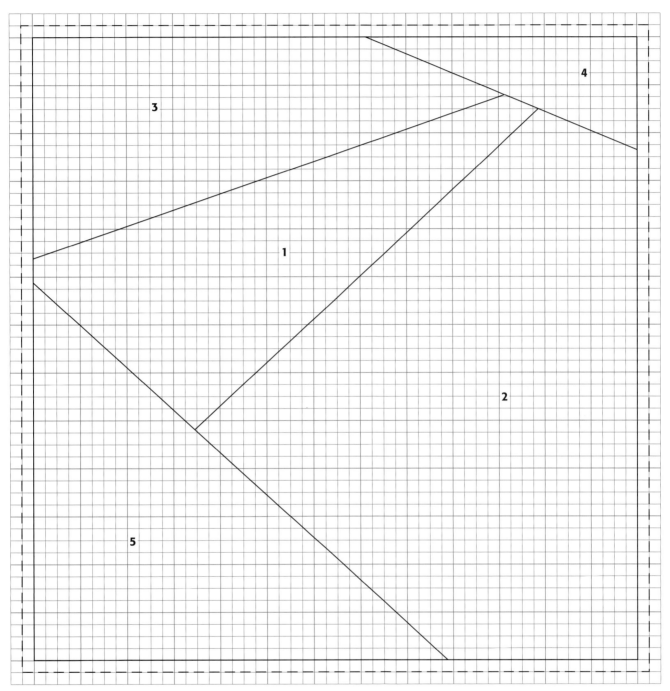

Enlarge pattern 200%.

1 square = ¼"

A FEW FLOWERS

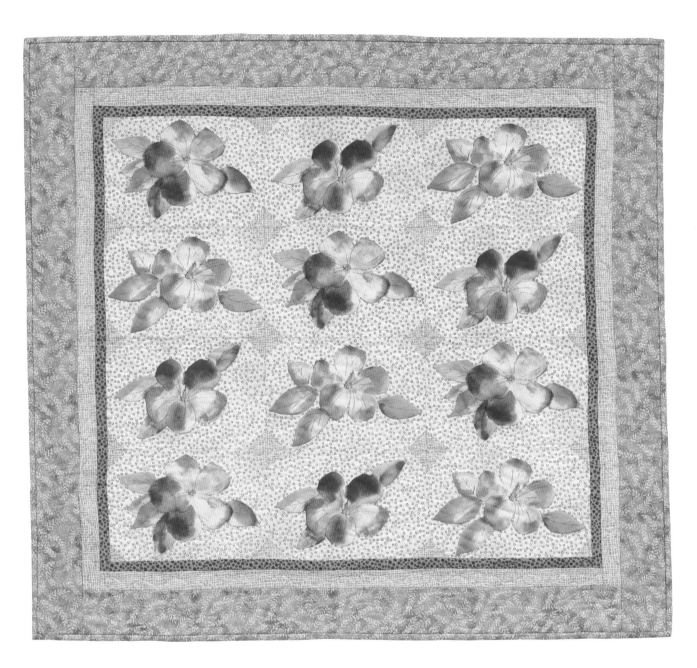

Sometimes the best plan for a stunning fabric is not to cut it . . . but to cut around it! A great way to use a Just Can't Cut It fabric is to cut out the motifs and appliqué them to your project, using the time-honored technique of *broderie perse* that was so popular more than a century ago. These enchanting flowers were cut from a magnificent floral print to create a delightful wall hanging in shades of peach and green.

Finished size: 35" x 32"

Designed and made by Jean Van Bockel

Materials

All yardages are based on 42"-wide fabric.

- 1 yd. cream print fabric for background
- ½ to 1 yd. Just Can't Cut It fabric for appliqués*
- ½ yd. green fabric for outside border
- ⅜ yd. pink fabric for middle border and background blocks
- ¼ yd. red fabric for inside border
- 1 yd. fabric for backing
- ½ yd. fabric for binding
- 40" x 36" piece of batting

*You will need 12 flowers that are approximately 8" x 6".

Cutting

From the pink fabric, cut:
- 5 strips, 1½" x 42"; crosscut into:
  - 2 strips, 1½" x 30½"
  - 2 strips, 1½" x 25½"
  - 48 squares, 1½" x 1½"

From the cream print fabric, cut:
- 3 strips, 6½" x 42"; crosscut into:
  - 12 pieces, 6½" x 9½"

From the red fabric, cut:
- 2 strips, 1" x 28½"
- 2 strips, 1" x 24½"

From the green fabric, cut:
- 2 strips, 3" x 27½"
- 2 strips, 3" x 35½"

From the binding fabric, cut:
- 4 strips, 2¾" x 42"

Assembly

1. On the wrong side of the pink squares, draw a diagonal line from corner to corner using a soft pencil and see-through ruler.

2. With right sides together, position 4 pink squares at the corners of each cream background piece. Stitch on the diagonal line. Trim the seam to ¼" and press the triangles toward the corners.

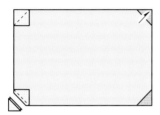

3. Referring to "Needle-Turn Appliqué" on page 73, cut out flower shapes from the Just Can't Cut It fabric, leaving a turn-under allowance of ¼" on all edges.

4. Position the flowers in the center of the background pieces from step 2. Use the needle-turn method to appliqué the flowers to the background.

Make 12.

5. Joining the short sides, sew the appliquéd blocks into 4 rows of 3 blocks each. Press.

6. Sew the 1" x 24½" red strips to the sides of the quilt top and press. Sew the 1" x 28½" red strips to the top and bottom. Press.

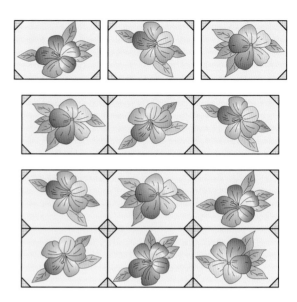

7. Sew the 1½" x 25½" pink strips to the sides of the quilt top and press. Sew the 1½" x 30½" pink strips to the top and bottom. Repeat to add the 3" x 27½" green strips to the sides and the 3" x 35½" green strips to the top and bottom.

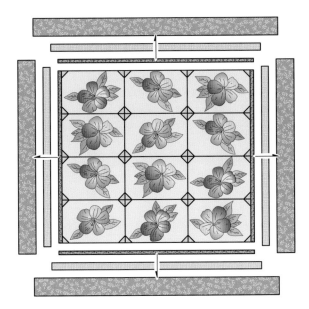

Finishing

1. Referring to "Finishing the Quilt Top" on pages 75–76, layer and baste the quilt. Stitch around the appliquéd flowers, ¹⁄₁₆" to ⅛" from the edges, and quilt the background, leaving the appliqués unquilted. Quilt the borders as desired.

2. Add binding to the quilt, referring to "Binding" on pages 77–78.

Referring to "Finishing the Quilt Top" on pages 75–76. "Binding" on pages 77–78.

FABRIC LOVER'S TIPS

For a different look, try making your quilt with bouquets rather than single blossoms. Create bouquets by grouping different flower motifs, or simply cut a floral spray from a lovely print. Or, if you prefer the look of just one flower per block but want variety, choose an assortment of flower motifs from different Just Can't Cut It fabrics.

Make a coordinating accessory or two to accompany the quilt wherever it's hanging. Using the remainder of your Just Can't Cut It fabric, make a simple throw pillow for a bed or sofa, or stitch up a few cloth napkins for your table.

FLORAL MOSAIC

This simple-to-make wall hanging is a great way to show off just about any charming Just Can't Cut It fabric. Large floral prints, Japanese yukatas, Dutch screen-printed fabrics, toiles, batiks, and African fabrics are all fair game. You may want to "fussy cut" your print so that you can place your favorite flower or other motif in the center squares.

Finished size: 39" x 39"

Materials

All yardages are based on 42"-wide fabric.

- 1 yd.* Just Can't Cut It fabric for the center squares
- ¾ yd. green print fabric for the outer border and corner triangles
- ½ yd. green check fabric for side setting triangles, center block, and narrow border
- ½ yd. dark green print fabric for side setting triangles and center block
- 1½ yds. fabric for backing
- ½ yd. fabric for binding
- 45" x 45" piece of batting
- See-through ruler
- Water-soluble marker

Purchase extra if you want to fussy cut your fabric.

Cutting

From the green check fabric, cut:
- 9 strips, 1½" x 42"

From the dark green print fabric, cut:
- 6 strips, 1½" x 42"
- 2 squares, 4½" x 4½"
- 1 square, 3½" x 3½"

From the Just Can't Cut It fabric, cut:
- 4 squares, 11½" x 11½"

From the green print fabric, cut:
- 2 squares, 8¾" x 8¾"; cut each square once diagonally
- 4 strips, 3½" x 42"

From the binding fabric, cut:
- 5 strips, 2¾" x 42"

FABRIC LOVER'S TIP

How about making more than one version of this quilt with seasonal, holiday, or theme fabrics? Change your quilt with the seasons!

Blocks

1. With right sides together and raw edges even, position one end of a green check strip at the top of a 4½" dark green print square. Stitch along the raw edges. Press and trim the strip even with the square as shown.

2. Repeat step 1 to add a green check strip to the right side of the unit.

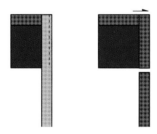

3. Repeat step 1 to add green check strips to the bottom and left side of the unit.

4. Repeat steps 1 through 3 to add a dark green strip to each side.

5. Add a second green check and dark green strip to each side to complete the block. The block will measure 12½" x 12½". Repeat to make a total of 2 blocks that will be used for the side setting triangles.

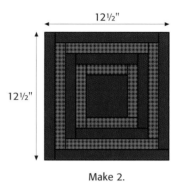

Make 2.

6. Working on the right side of the 2 blocks from step 5, draw a diagonal line from corner to corner with a pencil or water-soluble marker. Using a see-through ruler and rotary cutter, cut along this line to divide the blocks in half to make 4 side setting triangles.

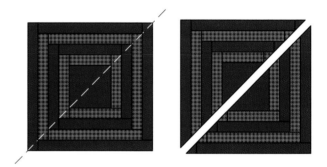

7. Beginning with the 3½" dark green print square, repeat steps 1 through 5 to make the center block. The block will measure 11½" x 11½".

Assembly

1. Sew into diagonal rows the 4 Just Can't Cut It squares, the center block from step 6, the side setting triangles from step 7, and the green print corner triangles. Sew the rows together to make the wall hanging center.

2. Refer to "Adding Borders" on pages 74–75. Measure the quilt top through the center to determine the length. Cut 2 green check border strips to that length and sew them to the sides of the quilt. Measure the quilt through the center to determine the width; cut 2 green check border strips to that width and sew them to the top and bottom of the quilt.

3. Repeat step 2 to add the outer green print border.

Finishing

1. Referring to "Finishing the Quilt Top" on pages 75–76, layer and baste the quilt. Machine quilt as desired, referring to "Just Can't Cut It Quilting" on page 76.

2. Add binding to the quilt, referring to "Binding" on pages 77–78.

FRENCH COUNTRY

If you have a weakness for those beautiful reproduction French toile fabrics, here's the perfect quilt.
Vintage French country quilts were my inspiration for this delicate-looking quilt made from a pastel toile print.
As a charming accent, appliquéd vines and leaves adorn the scalloped edges. For any special fabric that you want to let shine on
its own, this is the ideal design. I use this quilt on a table, but the size is appropriate for a twin-size bed, too.

Finished size: 66" x 85"

Materials

All yardages are based on 42"-wide fabric.

- 4¾ yds.* Just Can't Cut It fabric for center piece and outside border
- 1¼ yds. light green fabric for appliquéd vines and leaves
- ¾ yd. cream fabric for middle border
- ⅜ yd. dark pink fabric for narrow inside border
- 5¼ yds. for backing
- 1 yd. for binding
- 72" x 91" piece of batting
- ⅜" bias press bar
- Template plastic
- Freezer paper

Add an extra ½ yard for matching if you are using a large-scale print.

Cutting

From the dark pink fabric, cut:
- 3 strips, 1½" x 42"
- 2 strips, 1½" x 34½"

From the Just Can't Cut It fabric, cut:
- 1 piece, 32½" x 51½"
- 8 strips, 12½" x 42"

From the cream fabric, cut:
- 5 strips, 4½" x 42"

Assembly

1. Piece 3 dark pink 1½" x 42" strips and cut to make 2 border strips measuring 1½" x 51½". Sew to the sides of the 32½" x 51½" center piece of Just Can't Cut It fabric. Press toward the center. Sew the 1½" x 34½" dark pink strips to the top and bottom. Press.

2. Repeat step 1 to add 4½" x 53½" cream borders to the sides and 4½" x 42½" borders to the top and bottom. Press toward the dark pink border.

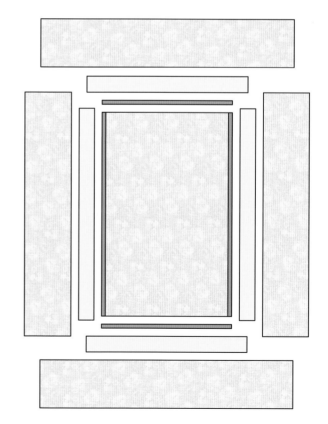

3. Sew the eight Just Can't Cut It strips together in pairs. Trim 2 of the strips to 61½" and sew to the sides. Press outward. Trim the remaining strips to 66½" and sew to the top and bottom. Press.

Scalloped Edge

1. Trace the scallop patterns on pages 68–69 onto template plastic and cut out. Cut 4 pieces of freezer paper, each approximately 8" wide and the length of each of the 4 sides of the quilt.

2. Beginning with the top border, trace the corner templates onto the dull side of the freezer paper. Trace and repeat the scallop template until you have joined the two corners with scallops. It may be necessary to overlap the template slightly for an even placement of the scallops.

Freezer paper

3. When you are pleased with the scallop placement, iron the freezer paper, shiny side down, onto the top of the quilt, matching the edges. Cut on the drawn line through the paper and fabric to create the scalloped edge.

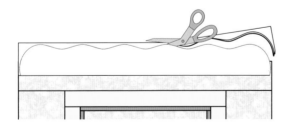

4. Using a strip of freezer paper you have cut the same length as the side, repeat to draw the scallop pattern for one side. When you position the freezer paper on the side of the quilt, overlap the corner sections and adjust slightly if necessary. Iron the paper to the quilt and cut out the side scallops.

5. Using the cut scallop from steps 3 and 4, trace the pattern onto the remaining two freezer-paper strips. Cut scallops on the bottom and remaining side of the quilt top, carefully overlapping each corner. Remove the freezer paper. Stay stitch around the edge of the quilt a scant ¼" from the scalloped edge.

Appliqué

1. Refer to "Cutting Bias Strips" on page 74. Cut approximately 375" of 1¼"-wide bias strips from the light green fabric.

2. Referring to "Appliqué Vines" on page 74, use the ⅜" bias press bar to make several long bias tubes from the strips. Cut the bias tubes into 22 vines measuring 12" long, and 14 shorter vines measuring 7" long.

3. Trace the leaf pattern from page 68 onto template plastic and cut it out. Referring to "Freezer-Paper Appliqué" on pages 72–73, trace the template onto freezer paper to make 224 leaves. Press them to the wrong side of the light green fabric.

4. Refer to the placement guide below to position the vines on the borders. You will have 4 short vines between 5 long vines on each side. On the top and bottom you will have 3 short vines between 4 long vines. At each corner, position 1 long vine to connect the vines on each side. To ensure a pleasing placement, position and pin the vines on one side before machine or hand appliquéing. Appliqué the vines; then arrange and appliqué the leaves.

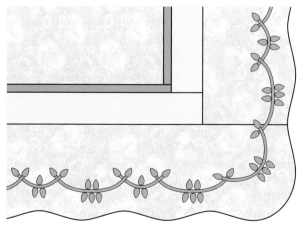

Appliqué Placement Guide

Finishing

1. Referring to "Finishing the Quilt Top" on pages 75–76, layer and baste the quilt. Outline quilt ⅛" to ¼" around the leaves and vines; then quilt as desired.

2. Add bias binding, referring to "Cutting Bias Strips" on page 74 and "Bias Binding" on page 78. Cut approximately 380" of 2¾"-wide bias strips.

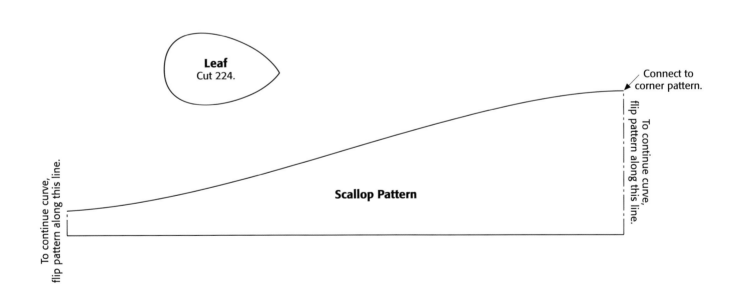

Leaf
Cut 224.

Connect to corner pattern.

To continue curve, flip pattern along this line.

Scallop Pattern

To continue curve, flip pattern along this line.

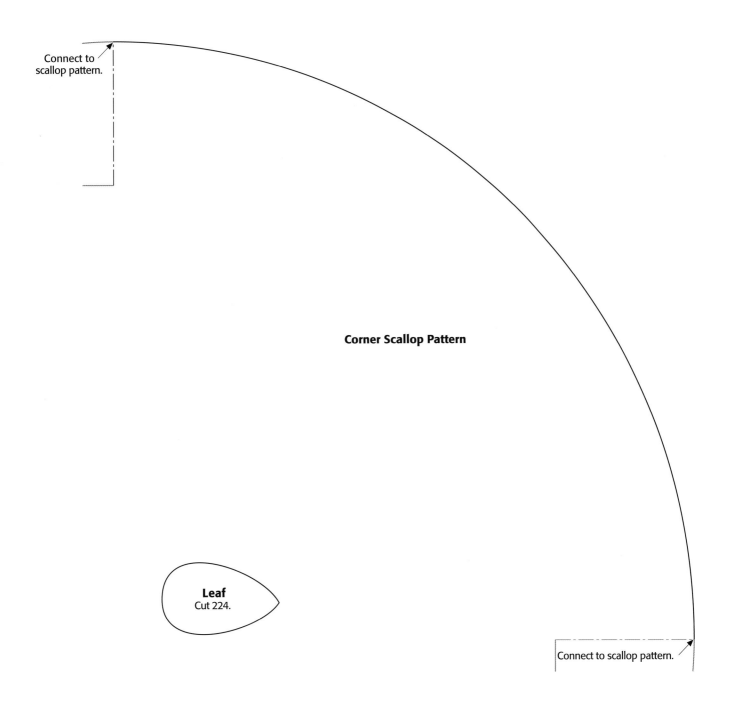

Connect to
scallop pattern.

Corner Scallop Pattern

Leaf
Cut 224.

Connect to scallop pattern.

THE ULTIMATE
JUST CAN'T CUT IT QUILT

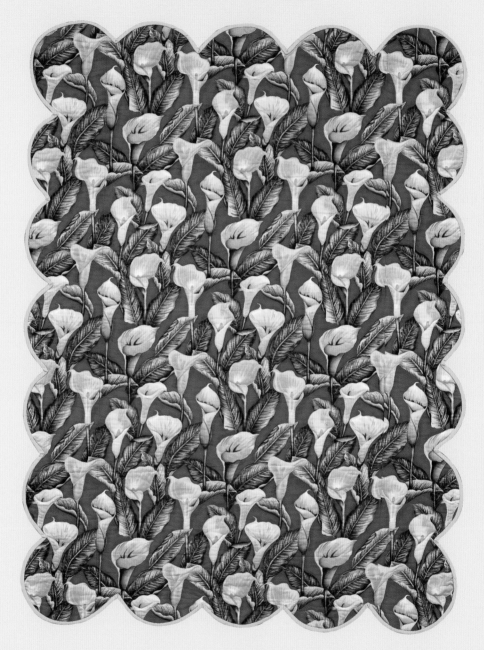

Finished size: 50" x 68"

If it's absolutely too gorgeous to cut at all—then don't! Like traditional whole-cloth quilts, this simple but dramatic variation of "French Country" uses a Just Can't Cut It fabric with a scalloped edge as a highlight. Add Just Can't Cut It quilting (see page 76) for a perfect finishing touch.

For this quilt, I used 4¼ yards of fabric.

1. Cut a center panel that is 68" x 42" or 68" by the width of the fabric. Cut the selvages from each side. Divide the remaining fabric in half lengthwise so that you have 2 sections, each approximately 21" wide.

2. Position 1 section to the left and the other to the right of the center panel, carefully matching the Just Can't Cut It print between the 3 sections. Move the side sections vertically and horizontally until the print matches. With right sides together, pin and sew the sections together.

3. Trim the top and bottom of the side panels so that they are even with the center panel. Trim the side panels to a width of 10" so that the width of the quilt is 50".

4. To make scallops the easy and accurate way, use a plate from the kitchen as a guide. Plates can be great quilting tools! Choose the size of the plate according to the width of the scallops you'd like. I usually use a 10" dinner plate as a tracing guide.

5. Referring to "Scalloped Edge," on page 66, cut freezer paper to the length of the quilt top. Place the plate at a corner of the freezer paper and trace around it to make the first scalloped corner. For the next scallop, overlap the first scallop by as much as you wish and then trace around the side of the plate. If you want a shallow scallop, overlap the plate tracings a great deal. If you prefer a deeper scallop, position and trace the plate farther from the preceding scallop. Continue around the quilt until you have a charming scalloped edge for your Just Can't Cut It quilt.

6. Refer to "Finishing the Quilt Top" on pages 75–76 and "Bias Binding" on page 78 to complete your almost instant quilt!

GENERAL DIRECTIONS

This chapter includes helpful instructions for completing the projects in this book. Refer to it often if you have questions about specific quiltmaking techniques. For further information on techniques, refer to "Resources" on page 79.

To make sure that you are pleased with your finished quilt, keep in mind a few important tips.

- Cut accurately and consistently, using the same brand of ruler throughout a project.
- Always stitch accurate ¼" seams.
- Press carefully after each stitching step in the instructions.

Appliqué

Various appliqué techniques can be used in the projects. I use freezer-paper appliqué and needle-turn appliqué most often, but you can easily adapt your favorite technique if you prefer.

Freezer-Paper Appliqué

Freezer paper, which is coated on one side, is often used as a template and stabilizer to help make perfectly shaped appliqués.

1. Trace the appliqué patterns *in reverse* on the dull (unwaxed) side of the freezer paper. Cut out the templates on the traced lines.

2. Place the freezer-paper template, shiny side down, on the *wrong side* of your chosen fabric and use a hot, dry iron to attach it to the fabric. Leave at least ¾" of space between pieces when ironing more than one freezer-paper template to the same fabric.

3. Cut out each shape, adding a ¼" seam allowance beyond the template edges. Clip inner curves and trim points to eliminate bulk.

4. Turn the seam allowance over the freezer-paper edge and press with the tip of an iron or secure the seam allowance with hand basting through the paper and both layers of fabric.

5. Pin or baste the appliqué onto the background fabric and sew in place using an appliqué stitch. Remove the basting stitches.

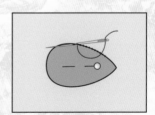

6. Carefully cut a slit in the background fabric behind the appliqué and remove the freezer paper with tweezers. If desired, trim away the background behind each appliqué, leaving a ¼" seam allowance all around.

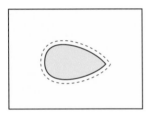

Back of appliqué

Needle-Turn Appliqué

1. Trace the appliqué patterns onto the dull (unwaxed) side of freezer paper. Cut out the templates on the traced lines.

2. Place the freezer-paper templates, shiny side down, on the *right side* of the fabric and use a hot, dry iron to press it onto the fabric. Leave at least ¾" of space between pieces when ironing more than one freezer-paper template to the same fabric.

3. Trace around each template with a pencil or fabric marker.

4. Cut out the appliqués, adding a scant ¼" turn-under allowance all around. Peel away the freezer-paper template.

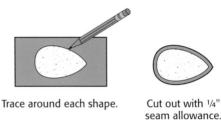

Trace around each shape. Cut out with ¼" seam allowance.

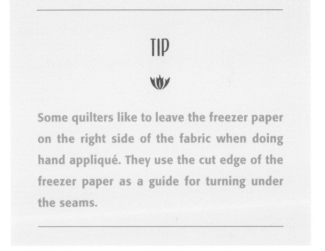

TIP

Some quilters like to leave the freezer paper on the right side of the fabric when doing hand appliqué. They use the cut edge of the freezer paper as a guide for turning under the seams.

5. Position the appliqués on the background fabric. Pin or baste in place.

6. Starting on a straight edge, use the tip of the needle to gently turn under the seam allowance along the marked line, about ½" at a time. Hold the turned seam allowance firmly between the thumb and first finger of one hand as you stitch the appliqué to the background fabric with your other hand. Use a longer needle—a Sharp or milliner's needle—to help you control the seam allowance and sweep it under neatly. Sew in place with the appliqué stitch. Clip the seam allowance as needed in curved areas.

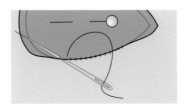

CUTTING BIAS STRIPS

Bias strips are cut across the diagonal of the fabric, on the bias. They are used for making appliqué tubes for vines and for binding curved-edge quilts.

To cut bias strips, place a single layer of fabric on a rotary-cutting mat. Using a ruler with a 45° angle marking, align the 45° angle marking with an edge of the fabric as shown. For binding, cut as many 2¾"-wide bias strips as you will need for your quilt. For appliquéd vines, cut the number and width of strips specified in the project instructions.

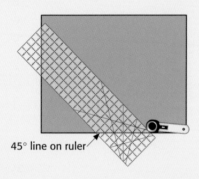

45° line on ruler

To create a long bias strip, join strips together end to end with a diagonal seam. Place strips right sides together, offsetting the seams by ¼" as shown. Stitch and press the seams open.

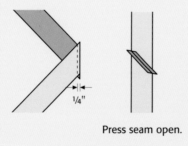

¼"

Press seam open.

Appliqué Vines

Making appliqué vines that curve gracefully is easy with the use of bias press bars, or bias bars. Bias bars are flat metal or nylon strips, available in a variety of widths.

1. Refer to "Cutting Bias Strips" at left and follow the project instructions to cut strips of the required length and width. Join the strips end to end with a diagonal seam.

2. Fold the bias strip in half lengthwise with wrong sides together. Measure from the fold a distance equal to the width of the required bias bar plus ⅛". Stitch this distance from the fold for the length of the bias strip, being very careful not to stretch the bias as you sew.

3. Trim the seam allowance to ⅛". Slip the appropriate bias bar into the fabric tube and adjust it so that the seam is centered on the bar. Steam press to flatten the tube, pressing the seam allowance to one side.

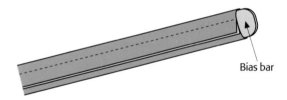

Bias bar

4. Remove the bias bar. Your vine is ready to pin or baste in position on the background fabric.

Adding Borders

1. Measure the length of the quilt top through the center. Cut the border strips to this measurement, piecing as necessary and using diagonal seams to join the strips.

2. Mark the center of the quilt edges and the border strips. Pin the border strips to the sides of the quilt top, matching the center marks and ends and easing as necessary. Sew the border strips in place and press the seams toward the border.

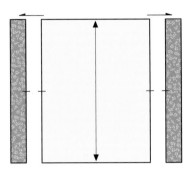

Measure center of quilt, top to bottom. Mark centers.

3. To determine the length of the top and bottom border strips, measure the width of the quilt top through the center, including the side border strips just added. Mark the centers, pin, and sew to the quilt. Press toward the border.

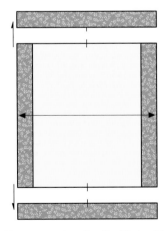

Measure center of quilt, side to side, including borders. Mark centers.

Finishing the Quilt Top

Determine how you will quilt your top and whether you need to mark the quilting design before layering the top with batting and backing. Marking is not necessary if you plan to quilt in the ditch (along the seam lines), outline quilt a uniform distance from seam lines, quilt a free-form meandering pattern using free-motion quilting, or use your Just Can't Cut It print as a quilting guide.

For complex or detailed quilting designs, mark the quilt top before layering the quilt. Use a marking tool that will be visible on your fabric. Test the marker on fabric scraps to be sure the marks can be removed easily.

Layering

Once the top is complete, give it one final pressing, making sure that the seams all go in the correct direction and that the top is smooth and flat. Then layer by making a quilt "sandwich" consisting of the backing, batting, and quilt top. I recommend cutting the quilt backing at least 3" to 4" larger than the quilt top on all sides.

For large quilts, it is usually necessary to sew two or three lengths of fabric together to make a backing of the required size. Trim away the selvage edges before sewing the lengths together. Press the backing seams open to make quilting easier.

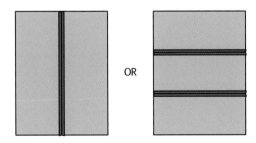

1. Lay the pressed backing on a clean, flat surface, wrong side up. Anchor it with masking tape, being careful not to stretch the fabric out of shape.

2. Spread the batting over the backing, smoothing out any wrinkles.

3. Center the pressed quilt top on the top of the batting with the right side up. Smooth out any wrinkles and make sure the quilt-top edges are parallel to the edges of the backing.

4. Baste with hand stitching or with safety pins.

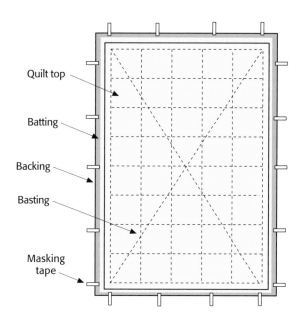

Quilt top

Batting

Backing

Basting

Masking tape

Just Can't Cut It Quilting

Choose your favorite quilting method to finish your project. All of the projects in this book were machine quilted. To further emphasize your fabulous Just Can't Cut It fabrics, I've included a few tips for quilting them.

Many beautiful Just Can't Cut It fabrics can inspire a perfect design for quilting. Use these gorgeous prints as the starting point for adding unique quilting designs to your treasured project. Study your print and decide how to best emphasize the lines in it. Or think about how you will be using the fabric in the design of your quilt. For instance, if you are making a quilt with horizontal lines, such as "I Love Liberty" (page 23), then add quilting in a horizontal pattern.

Using the outline and details of the fabric as a quilting guide will give a distinctive touch to your quilt and further enhance the beauty of the print. Keep these easy tips in mind for perfect Just Can't Cut It quilting:

1. Set your stitch length to slightly longer than you normally use.

2. Drop the feed dogs on your machine and attach a darning foot or walking foot. This will allow you to do free-motion quilting and to follow the curves and details of the fabric.

3. Use a thread color that blends with the fabric. If you plan to outline quilt the fabric motifs, using a thread that contrasts with the fabric will only emphasize any slight stitching imperfections.

4. Simplify the design shown on the fabric. It isn't necessary to quilt along all the lines. Choose the major lines of the design to outline; then add a few details.

5. When quilting on the background, stitch slightly outside the outline of the print. If you use a thread color that blends into the background, any imperfections in your outline quilting will blend into the background but still accent your Just Can't Cut It fabric. Don't forget to add a few accent lines of quilting within the design as well. Just try to stitch on areas that match or blend well with your thread color.

Binding

Straight-Cut Binding

Binding cut straight across the width of the fabric is fine for most quilts with straight edges and 90° corners. For a French double-fold binding, cut strips as directed in the project. Binding strips cut at 2¾" will result in a finished binding about ½" wide. For a narrower binding, cut strips to the width desired. I prefer the wider binding so that it lies flat and does not look rounded.

1. With right sides together, sew the binding strips together on the diagonal as shown to create one long strip. Trim the excess fabric and press the seams open.

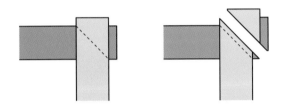

2. Fold the strip in half lengthwise, wrong sides together, and press. Turn under ¼" at a 45° angle at one end of the strip and press.

Fold line

3. Beginning on one side of the quilt and using a ¼" seam allowance, stitch the binding to the quilt, keeping the raw edges even with the edge of the quilt top. Use a walking foot if you have one, to feed the layers through the machine evenly. Stop stitching ¼" from the corner of the quilt and backstitch. Clip the thread.

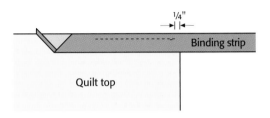

¼"

Binding strip

Quilt top

4. Turn the quilt so you will be stitching down the next side. Fold the binding up, away from the quilt and then back down onto itself, keeping the raw edges even. Begin stitching at the edge, backstitch, and continue to the next corner, stopping ¼" from the end. Repeat the process for the corners and remaining sides.

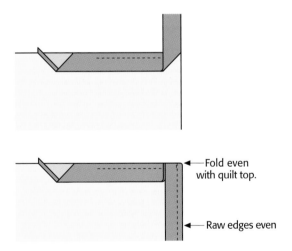

Fold even with quilt top.

Raw edges even

5. When you reach the starting point, lap the strip over the beginning stitches by about 1" and cut away any excess binding, trimming the end at a 45° angle. Tuck the end of the binding into the fold and complete the seam.

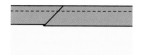

6. Fold the binding over the raw edges to the back, covering the row of machine stitching. Blindstitch the binding in place, mitering the corners.

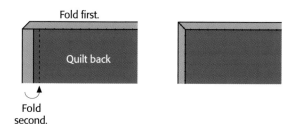

Bias Binding

Plaid and striped fabrics look especially dramatic when they are cut on the bias and used for bindings. It is also necessary to cut binding strips on the bias when you are binding a quilt with curved or scalloped edges such as "French Country" (page 64) or "The Ultimate Just Can't Cut It Quilt" (page 70).

To add bias bindings, refer to "Cutting Bias Strips" on page 74 and cut 2¾"-wide bias strips until you have cut the total number of inches given in the project instructions. To create one long strip, sew the strips together with diagonal seams.

After you have cut and pieced the bias strips, refer to "Straight-Cut Binding" on pages 77–78 and follow steps 1 through 6 to add the binding to your quilt.

RESOURCES

Here are a few of my favorite books. Some of them are excellent references for quilting techniques while others are beautiful books offering wonderful projects and endless inspiration!

Barnes, Christine. *Color: The Quilter's Guide*. Bothell, Wash.: Martingale & Company, 1997.

England, Kaye and Mary Elizabeth Johnson. *Quilt Inspirations from Africa*. Chicago: The Quilt Digest Press, 2000.

Fassett, Kaffe. *Patchwork and Quilting, Book Number 1*. Amherst, N. H.: Westminster Fibers, Inc., 1999.

———. *Patchwork and Quilting, Book Number 2*. Amherst, N. H.: Westminster Fibers, Inc., 2000.

Noble, Maurine. *Machine Quilting Made Easy*. Bothell: Wash.: That Patchwork Place, 1994.

Pippen, Kitty. *Quilting with Japanese Fabrics*. Bothell, Wash.: Martingale & Company, 2000.

Smith, Louisa L. *Strips 'n Curves: A New Spin on Strip Piecing*. Lafayette, Calif.: C&T Publishing, 2001.

Townswick, Jane. *Artful Appliqué the Easy Way*. Bothell, Wash.: Martingale & Company, 2000.

ABOUT THE AUTHOR

Pamela Mostek has loved making pretty things for as long as she can remember. She has experimented with and created in a wide variety of media including watercolor, decorative painting, weaving, and fabric surface design. If it involves fashioning something beautiful, she has probably given it a try!

One of her absolute favorite passions is for gorgeous fabrics. Ever since she began quilting fifteen years ago, she has particularly loved collecting special, fantastic prints. Having an incredible collection of fabulous and exotic fabrics that she hesitated to cut into was the inspiration for *Just Can't Cut It*.

Putting her degree in art and journalism to good use, she spends her time creating quilts for books and for her pattern company, Making Lemonade Designs. Pam is a proud mother of two grown daughters and grandmother of three very special grandchildren. She and her husband reside in Cheney, Washington.